Fundamentals of Craps

By

Mason Malmuth and Lynne Loomis

A product of Two Plus Two Publishing

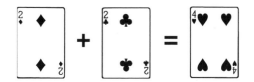

SECOND EDITION
First Printing
May 2004

Printing and Binding
Creel Printing Co.
Las Vegas, Nevada

Printed in the United States of America

Fundamentals of Craps

For information contact: **Two Plus Two Publishing, LLC**
600 West Sunset
Suite 103
Henderson, NV 89015
(702) 896-1326
www.twoplustwo.com

ISBN: 1-880685-30-2

Dedicated to the Memory of

Walter I. Nolan

(1924-1987)

Walter I. Nolan, whose initials form the acronym WIN, was the pen name of the late John Luckman, the founder of Gambler's Book Club. During his illustrious career, Luckman not only wrote numerous books and pamphlets on various gambling topics, but also was directly responsible for bringing to life many additional top-quality works by other gaming authors. He is remembered for his integrity, his adherence to high standards, and his devotion to both the publishing and gaming industries.

It was with the hope of following the tradition established by John Luckman that the Fundamentals of Craps *was written, and it is with honor and reverence that this booklet is dedicated to the memory of his literary pseudonym, Walter I. Nolan.*

Table of Contents

Introduction

Craps has the deserved reputation of being the fastest and most exciting table game offered by casinos. At first glance, it also appears to be extremely complicated, which is why many potential players are intimidated and afraid to try it. However, craps is surprisingly simple and easy to learn.

The game is also a good gamble, providing you know which bets to make. While many bets that you have the option of making carry a high house percentage, the standard bets on the craps layout are some of the best wagers available in casinos. Nevertheless, in the long run, craps is not a beatable casino game. No matter what you may hear — and regardless of which bets you make or how you make them — if you play craps long enough, you can expect to lose your money.

This doesn't mean that craps is not a skilled game. The skill comes in knowing which bets to make — that is, how to minimize the house advantage for any given amount of money that you wager — and which bets to stay away from, since the high house percentage craps bets are some of the worst bets in a casino. By the same token, like all casino games, craps contains a great deal of short-term luck. This fact, coupled with the low house edge on many bets, will give you a reasonable chance of leaving the table a winner after a short playing session.

Moreover, craps is a congenial form of gambling that promotes an us-against-them camaraderie. The game can be incredibly noisy at times — especially if a hot hand develops — and it's common to hear players around a dice table yell and cheer, as the shooter makes point after point and the right bettors take the money down.

Although you may not know right now what we mean by "hot hand," "point after point," and "right bettors," it won't be long

2 Fundamentals of Craps

before these terms become familiar. Keep reading — and good luck at the craps tables.

A Brief History

When and where the game of craps originated is unknown. However, dice have been around for as long as recorded history and have been found in the ruins of many ancient civilizations. In fact, there is even evidence that prehistoric man played games with a six-sided bone that probably was the forerunner of today's modern dice.

In the 18th century, a game called "Hazard" gained noticeable popularity in England. Hazard was very similar to modern-day craps, except that the shooter had some additional options that are not available today. Most significant is that in Hazard, the numbers 2, 3, and 12 were known as "crabs."

During the early 1800s, craps was introduced into the United States at the port of New Orleans. By the time the game arrived in this country, it was played pretty much as it is today. But the American population — never a stickler for the Queen's English — began to mispronounce "crabs," and the name "craps" subsequently evolved.

Craps was widely played in private games during the 19th century, but it did not appear very often on the Mississippi steam ships or in the great gambling halls of the Old West. A primary reason for this was that craps was a one-way game in which the dice could be bet only to win. Consequently, players were suspicious and feared that loaded (or unfair) dice would be introduced into the game and used against them.

Then in the early 1900s, dicemaker John Winn introduced a 5 percent commission, or vigorish, for don't pass bets. The commission was necessary, as otherwise players would have an advantage over the house on these bets. The 5 percent vig enabled craps to become a two-way game, and since the house now had an incentive to keep the dice honest, players overcame their initial misgivings.

4 Fundamentals of Craps

It wasn't long before a variation of the 5 percent commission evolved and became popular. By barring the ace-deuce — that is, this particular combination of dice would neither win nor lose — a player could make a don't pass bet without paying the house vig. It soon became apparent, however, that the ace-deuce came up too often, so casinos modified this feature to the Bar-12 or Bar-2 positions that we know today.

Because of this innovative change, craps soared in popularity, and thanks to the enthusiasm of U.S. servicemen during World War II, the game is now played worldwide. Nevertheless, craps is known as a uniquely American game and enjoys its greatest popularity in the modern casinos of the United States.

Getting Started

The Craps Layout

The playing surface of a craps table, which is known as the layout, may appear complex to someone unfamiliar with the game. However, the layout has nothing to do with the actual mechanics of playing craps. The various boxes, numbers, dice illustrations, and so forth serve only as an easy and convenient way for both the dealers and the players to keep track of all the bets. In fact, the layout has often been referred to as the "road map" of the game, in that each player at a craps table has designated locations on the layout where his bets are placed, either by himself or by the dealer, depending on the type of wager made.

We won't cover the details of the layout here, as these are discussed later in the *Fundamentals of Craps* in the various sections on individual bets. However, there are two things you should keep in mind. First, the left side of the layout is identical to the right side, except for the proposition bets in the center. This means that the layout is, at worst, only half as complicated as it may appear. Second, those proposition bets — which are wagers that specific sides of the dice will come up together — have a very high house percentage. Consequently, if you ignore them, you not only will have less to worry about, but also will not be making any bets where you have an enormous disadvantage.

The Crew

The casino personnel who run a craps game are referred to collectively as "the crew." There are usually four members of this crew: the boxman, two dealers, and the stickman.

6 Fundamentals of Craps

The boxman sits at the center of the table between the two dealers. His primary duties are to guard against errors and to settle any disputes that may arise. As the crew member in charge of the game, the boxman supervises all operations and monetary transactions. He also periodically examines the dice in play.

The dealers are responsible for selling chips to the players and for handling all bets, with the exception of the proposition bets in the center of the table. Besides collecting and paying the bets on his side of the layout, the dealer also takes care of placing the "dice buck" (sometimes called a "puck"), which is a round marker used to indicate the point number and to show that the odds are off on the come-out roll.

The final member of the four-person crew is the stickman, who directs the game and sets its tempo. He controls the dice with a long curved stick, pushing them to the player whose turn it is to "shoot" and retrieving them after each roll. In addition, the stickman announces each number as it is rolled and takes care of the proposition bets in the center of the layout.

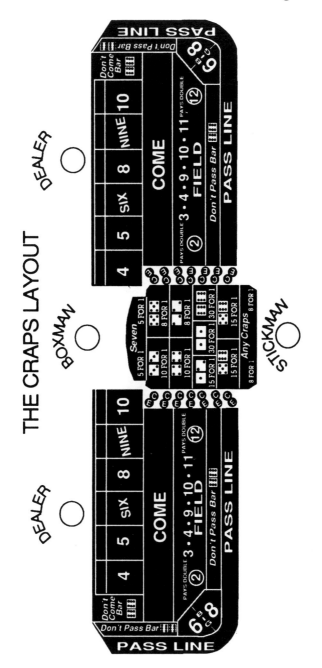

THE CRAPS LAYOUT

A Little Math

Before we discuss the various bets in craps, it is important that you become familiar with the underlying mathematics of the game, which is relatively easy to understand.

A die is a perfect six-sided cube. Each side of the cube is marked with from one to six spots, and the opposing sides always total seven. Since a die is perfectly balanced, each of the six sides has an equal probability — that is, one chance in six — of landing face up when the die is rolled. In other words, the side with three spots is just as likely to land face up as the side with four spots.

When a second die is added to the first — making a pair of dice — each individual die rolls independently of the other, and each can land face up on one of six sides. Consequently, since the first die has six possible outcomes, and since the second die can come up six different ways in combination with each outcome of the first die, there are 36 (6 x 6) equally likely results that a pair of dice can produce.

However, the 36 possible outcomes are spread over only 11 possible totals. For example, the numbers 6 and 1 and the numbers 4 and 3 both produce a total of 7, yet each of these combinations is a different one of the 36 possible results.

The chart on the following page illustrates the 36 possible outcomes produced by two dice and also shows the chances that each of the 11 numbers has of coming up when the dice are rolled.

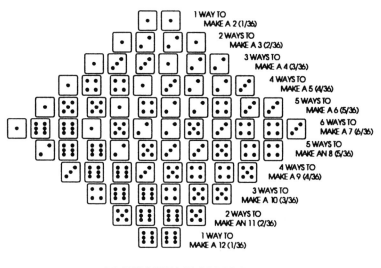

36 POSSIBLE OUTCOMES

How often each of the 11 possible numbers appears is the basis for the game of craps. This establishes the odds associated with the various wagers available, which in turn determine the casino payoffs on winning bets.

The Basics of Play

As we stated earlier, even though craps may look complicated to a novice, the game is actually easy to play. Craps revolves around the player holding the dice — who is referred to as the shooter — and everyone at the table essentially is betting either for or against him. That is, every player is wagering either that the shooter will make a pass and win or that he will fail to make a pass and thus lose.

As an example, let's suppose you are playing craps and it's your turn to shoot. You first will place a bet either on the pass line — wagering that you will win — or on the don't pass line, which is a wager that you will lose. There are, of course, many bets in addition to this one that you can make, but to shoot the dice, you must bet either the pass line or the don't pass line.

Once you have placed your bet, the stickman will push you anywhere from five to eight dice, and you will choose two of them to throw. It doesn't matter which ones you select, since all casino dice are made to exact specifications and for all practical purposes are identical.

Let's assume that you have bet the pass line. If you throw a total of 7 or 11 on your first roll, which is known as the come-out roll, you have made a pass and will win your bet, which is paid at even money. If you roll any craps — which is a total of 2, 3, or 12 — you will lose your bet.

If any other total (4, 5, 6, 8, 9, or 10) appears on the come-out roll, you have established a point and will now continue to shoot the dice until you either repeat the point number or throw a total of 7. If you repeat the point number before rolling a 7, you again have made a pass, and your pass line bet will be paid at even money. However, if a 7 comes up before your point number is repeated, you have sevened-out and will lose your bet.

Once a point has been established, only that point number or a 7 will determine whether you win or lose your pass line bet. Any other numbers that you may roll in the interim — including the 11 and the 2, 3, and 12 craps numbers — have no bearing on this particular wager, although they do affect other bets that can be made in a craps game. (These are discussed later in the booklet.)

As you no doubt have surmised by now, when your pass line bet wins, wagers on the don't pass line lose, and vice versa. Thus, if you throw a craps on the come-out roll or seven-out before repeating your point number, you and all other pass line bettors will lose, while those players who bet the don't pass will win.

In addition, you must relinquish the dice when you seven-out. As before, the stickman will then push several dice to the next player in a clockwise rotation around the table, and the new shooter will select two of them to throw. Note that you do not give up the dice when you roll a craps on the come-out, even though your pass line bet loses. You will throw the dice again for a new come-out roll and will continue doing so until you have established a point number. Only when you roll a seven before repeating that point number do you relinquish the dice.

Also note that you do not have to throw the dice when it's your turn to shoot. Simply tell the stickman that you wish to pass the dice, and he will push them to the next player in turn.

Right Bets

Introduction

As previously mentioned, the game of craps offers some of the best bets in a casino. Specifically, these bets have either a very low house edge or no house edge at all. This is what makes craps a "good gamble" and is why it is the favorite game of many people who regularly visit a gaming center.

In this section, we will cover the pass line bet in greater detail, as well as discuss the come bet. Both of these wagers are known as "right bets." We also will cover taking the odds, which is a bet with no house advantage that nonetheless is still offered by a casino.

Incidentally, when we refer to craps as a "good gamble," we don't mean that you have the best of it but that because of the low house edge, you will have a reasonable chance of walking away from the table a winner for any short session you may play. But as we've stated, if you play dice long enough, you cannot expect to beat the game.

The Pass Line Bet

When it is your turn to throw the dice, you must determine whether to bet the pass line or the don't pass line. Most shooters, as well as most of the other players at the table, will bet the pass line, as it is the basic wager of craps.

The pass line wager is an even money bet that wins if you either roll a total of 7 or 11 — sometimes called a "natural" — on the come-out roll, or if you throw a 4, 5, 6, 8, 9, or 10 on the come-out roll and repeat that number, which is referred to as a "point," before you roll a 7. The pass line bet loses if the come-out roll is a 2, 3, or 12 — known as "craps" — or when a 7 is rolled before the established point number is repeated.

If you successfully complete a pass — that is, if you repeat an established point number before throwing a 7 — you get to roll the dice again. Only when you seven-out will the stickman push the dice to the next player in succession.

Once you have established a point, if you roll a number other than your point or a 7, it is disregarded as far as pass line bets are concerned (although as noted earlier, these additional rolls do affect other bets that can be made at the craps table). Moreover, it doesn't matter how long it takes to complete your pass or seven-out.

As an example, suppose you have established a point of 8 on the come-out roll. If you next throw a 3, then a 5, a 9, and a 10, these numbers will be ignored for pass line bets. But if you then roll a 7, you will lose your pass line wager, since the 7 came up before your point number.

You can expect to win the pass line bet 488 times out of 990 decisions, which means that you will lose this bet 502 times. These additional 14 decisions in favor of the house give the casino an advantage of 1.41 percent. In other words, out of every $100 that you wager, you can expect to lose $1.41.

To determine a line decision in craps requires, on average, 3.38 rolls of the dice. However, one-third of the time, your bet — win or lose — will be decided on the come-out roll; that is, the shooter will throw a 7, an 11, or one of the craps numbers. Put another way, out of the 36 possible outcomes produced by a pair of dice, 12 of them will be composed of the aforementioned numbers. (There are six ways to roll a 7, two ways to roll an 11, and four ways to throw a craps number, for a total of 12 outcomes.) Two-thirds of the time, a new shooter will establish a point, and occasionally he will have to roll the dice numerous times before a pass line decision is made.

When a shooter holds the dice for an extended period of time before either making his point or rolling a 7, he is said to have a "long hand." A shooter is said to have a "hot hand" when he not only holds the dice for a long time, but also makes numerous passes.

A pass line bet can be made at any time during a shooter's hand, even after he has established a point. However, a bet placed on the pass line after a point has been established is a very poor wager, since you have missed the opportunity to win on the come-out roll when the shooter throws a 7 or an 11. The only way you can now win is if the shooter repeats his point before he sevens-out.

Note that once a pass line bet has been placed, it cannot be removed from the craps layout until a line decision has been determined. When the pass line wins, you can then pick up your original bet, plus your winnings; when this bet loses, the dealer will retrieve your wager.

Taking the Odds

When the shooter establishes a point on the come-out roll, any player who has made a pass line bet is allowed to "take the odds." A single odds bet is an additional wager, up to the amount of your original wager, that the point number will be repeated before a 7 is rolled.

The odds bet is the best wager you can make in the game of craps, because the house has no built-in advantage. Some casinos permit players to make double odds, triple odds, and even greater odds wagers. (As this booklet is being written, we know of two casinos in Nevada that offer 10 times odds on bets at the craps tables. In addition, we know of two Nevada casinos that periodically have offered as much as 100 times odds in their dice games.)

The odds bet not only has no "juice" associated with it, but also has no official designated space on the dice table. Therefore, to take the odds, you must place the appropriate amount of chips behind your pass line bet in the open area of the craps layout.

The correct payoff for odds bets varies from point number to point number, depending on the odds of a 7 being rolled before a particular point is repeated. The payoff formula is the same whether you take single odds, double odds, triple odds, or so forth. Correct odds payoffs are as follows:

- Points 4 and 10 pay 2-to-1

- Points 5 and 9 pay 3-to-2

- Points 6 and 8 pay 6-to-5

As an example, suppose you bet $1 on the pass line and establish a point of 4 in a casino that offers double odds. You now have the option of taking the odds for an additional $2. (You also can wager a lesser amount or, of course, choose not to take any odds at all.) If you repeat your point number before rolling a 7, you will get your original $3 back, plus an additional $5. Of that $5, $1 will be the even-money payback on your pass line wager, and $4 will be the 2-to-1 payoff for a point of 4 on your odds bet of $2. If you roll a 7 before repeating your point of 4, you will lose your initial $1 wager on the pass line, plus your $2 odds bet, for a total loss of $3.

We have said that the odds bet is a wager that carries no house advantage. Another way of putting this is that taking the odds effectively lowers the house edge on the total amount of money you have put in action. Specifically, if you take single odds on your pass line bet, instead of bucking the casino's advantage of

1.41 percent, you will be up against a house edge of 0.85 percent on your total wager. (Remember, your total wager is the amount you have bet on the pass line, plus the amount you have bet to take the odds.) If you take double odds, the house edge is now reduced to 0.61 percent on your total wager. And in those cases that allow you to take more than double odds, the house edge on your total wager will be less than one-half of 1 percent.

You are allowed to remove your odds wager from the craps table at any time, as a casino does not object to your taking down a bet that has no house edge. However, as noted previously, your original pass line bet cannot be removed until a line decision has been determined. Once a point has been established, the casino has a large advantage on pass line wagers and requires that these bets remain in action.

When taking the odds, you must keep in mind that a casino will not make change for less than the minimum bet. Suppose, for instance, that you are playing craps at a $1 minimum table and that single odds wagers are permitted. If you bet $1 on the pass line, establish a point of 6, bet an additional $1 by taking the 6-to-5 odds, and then make your point, you will receive a total payoff of only $2 instead of the $2.20 that is due you. This is because the casino cannot make change for $1, as it does not have smaller denomination chips available on the table. However, if your original line bet were $5 in this situation and you took the odds for an additional $5, you would receive the correct total payoff of $11.

If you have difficulty at the craps table in determining the proper amount to bet in order to receive the correct odds payoff, feel free to ask one of the dealers for assistance. You don't want to lose out on any winnings that are rightfully yours.

How to Bet

Let's say that you are playing craps in a casino that offers single odds and that you have decided to make $10 bets on the pass line. By betting this way, you will lose an average of 14 cents every time you make a pass line wager.

Instead of using this strategy, we recommend that you bet $5 on the pass line and take the odds for an additional $5 every time a point is established. Notice that you will have the same $10 in action. However, instead of facing that 1.41 percent house advantage, you now will be up against an edge of only 0.85 percent. As a result, you can expect your money to last almost twice as long, which means that you will have twice as many opportunities to catch a hot hand and leave the table a winner.

Come Bets

A come bet is identical to a pass line bet, with one exception: A come bet may be made on every throw of the dice once the shooter has established a point. A come bet is made by placing the amount of chips you wish to wager in the designated come area of the craps layout.

After you have placed a come bet, the very next throw of the dice becomes the come-out roll for that wager. Thus if the shooter rolls a 7, you will win even though pass line bettors will lose. If an 11 is rolled, you will win while the line bets will not be affected. Conversely, should one of the craps numbers come up, you will lose but the line bets will be unaffected.

Should the shooter throw one of the box numbers on the first roll of the dice after you've made a wager on the come, this number becomes an established point for your come bet. To win this bet, your come point must be repeated before a 7 is rolled. As an example, if the shooter throws a 6 on the initial roll, he must repeat the 6 before rolling a 7 for you to win this wager. Note that if the shooter makes a pass — that is, if he repeats the point established for pass line bettors — the next throw of the dice is just another roll in your come bet sequence, even though it is a new come-out roll for pass line bettors.

Once a point has been established for your come bet, the dealer will move the chips you have wagered to the corresponding numbered box on the craps layout to await a decision for that point. When you win a come bet, the dealer will pay you off by placing your original wager, along with your winnings, in the come section of the layout. If you do not immediately retrieve your chips, they will be in action on the next roll of the dice as a new come bet.

The house advantage on come bets is identical to that for pass line bets. However, you are permitted to take the same amount of odds on come bets as you are on pass line wagers, and these odds bets will have the same effect of reducing the overall house edge on your total wager.

To make an odds wager on a come point, hand the dealer the appropriate amount of chips and tell him that you wish to take the odds on that point. The dealer will then place your odds wager on top of your come bet as illustrated, which enables him to distinguish one bet from the other.

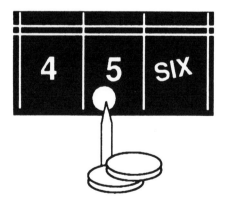

As with odds wagers on pass line bets, you are permitted to remove your odds wagers on come points at any time. Simply tell the dealer, "Odds off." In most casinos, the odds bets on come points are automatically off on the come-out roll. Should you wish these odds bets to remain in action on the come-out, you should inform the dealer, "Odds working."

If you make a lot of come bets, there will be times when you have most of the numbers on the table covered. It can be disheartening if the shooter then rolls a 7 and all of your bets — except your next come bet — lose. However, if the shooter has a long hand — that is, if he throws many point numbers before he sevens-out — you will collect money on each roll of the dice, ensuring a big score in a short period of time.

Walter I. Nolan once described a come bet as being "a game within a game." So if you make numerous come bets, you essentially will be playing lots of separate games within a game. This will not change the overall house advantage, but the action will be fast and furious. And when a hot hand develops, craps becomes extremely exciting and a great deal of fun to play.

If you are new to craps, we recommend that you not make too many come bets at one time, as the action can be confusing to a novice player. Start out by making a pass line bet with odds and perhaps one come bet with odds. Only when you feel comfortable with the game and are able to easily follow the action should you make additional wagers on the come.

Wrong Bets

Introduction

Another class of low house percentage wagers that the game of craps offers are the don't pass line bet and the don't come bet, both of which are referred to as "wrong bets."

Just as with right bets, you are permitted to make odds wagers in conjunction with wrong bets. However, in this case, you must lay the odds instead of taking them. (As noted in the previous section, odds wagers are offered by a casino even though these bets have no built-in house advantage.)

The majority of craps players — in fact, more than 90 percent — do not make wrong bets, although there's nothing worse about these wagers. It's just that the typical player likes to root for the shooter to win rather than to lose — especially if he happens to be the shooter.

The Don't Pass Line Bet

As you've seen, a pass line bet is simply a wager that the shooter will win. But you also can bet that the shooter will fail to make a pass and thus lose. To make a don't pass line bet, which pays even money, just place your chips in the space provided on the craps layout.

The don't pass line bet wins when the shooter throws a craps of 2 or 3, but not 12, on the come-out roll, or when he rolls a 7 before repeating his established point number. This wager loses when the come-out roll is a 7 or 11, or when the shooter repeats his point number before rolling a 7.

Notice that a don't pass line bet is the exact opposite of a pass line bet, with one exception: Although a roll of 12 on the come-out loses for pass line bettors, it is not a winning number for don't pass bettors. It is a stand-off; that is, it neither wins nor loses. The reason for this is simple: If don't bettors were permitted to win in this situation, they would have an advantage over the house. So by barring — or disallowing — the number 12 on the come-out roll, casinos retain a small edge. (Some casinos bar the number 2, but the effect is exactly the same.)

The house advantage on a don't pass line bet is 1.40 percent, as opposed to 1.41 percent on a pass line bet. This means that for every $100 you wager on the don't pass, you can expect to lose $1.40, which is a savings of 1 cent for the same amount of action as on the pass line. You obviously can play a great deal of craps before you ever notice this minuscule difference.

Unlike a pass line wager, which must remain in action to conclusion, a don't pass bet can be removed after a point number (4, 5, 6, 8, 9, or 10) has been established on the come-out roll. This is because you now have an advantage over the house, thus the casino has no objections to your taking down the bet. Of course, you should never do this. After going up against an 8-to-3 house edge on the come-out roll (eight ways to make a 7 or 11 versus three ways to make a 2 or 3), you will have an overall average advantage of 18.8 percent after a point has been established. Consequently, don't pass wagers should always remain in action until a line decision is determined.

Laying the Odds

When the shooter establishes a point number on the come-out roll, players who have made don't pass line wagers are permitted to lay the odds, which is exactly the opposite of taking the odds.

For example, let's suppose the shooter has established a point of 4. When you *take* the odds and win your bet, you will receive $2 for every $1 you have wagered, since the odds of throwing a 7 before a 4 is rolled are 2-to-1. By the same token, when you *lay* the odds and win your bet, you will receive $1 for every $2 you have bet, as making a 7 is twice as likely as making a 4.

If you choose to lay the odds, you don't have to lay the maximum amount allowed. However, the payoff formula is the same whether you lay single odds, double odds, or higher odds. Correct payoffs for lay odds bets are as follows:

- Points 4 and 10 pay 1-to-2

- Points 5 and 9 pay 2-to-3

- Points 6 and 8 pay 5-to-6

The craps layout has no official designated space for laying the odds, nor does it have an open area next to the don't pass section. Therefore, when you wish to make this bet, hand your chips to the dealer and inform him that you are laying the odds. The dealer will then place your odds wager on top of your don't pass line bet as shown in the illustration.

Laying the odds on don't pass line bets — like taking the odds on pass line wagers — reduces the casino's advantage on the total amount of money you've put in action. If you lay single odds, the house edge is lowered from 1.40 percent to 0.69 percent. And by laying double odds on your don't pass line bets, you will reduce the house advantage to 0.46 percent, which is less than one-half of 1 percent on your total wager.

You are permitted to remove your lay odds bet at any time. Again, this is because a casino doesn't object to your retrieving a wager that has no built-in house edge.

How to Bet

As we stated earlier, when you are playing craps in a casino that offers odds, you should reduce your pass line bet and make up the difference in your total wager by taking the odds. Betting in this manner enables you to put the same amount of money in action but reduces the house edge on your total bet. Similar strategy is recommended when playing the don't pass line. That is, you should make an appropriate smaller bet and then lay the odds.

Let's suppose, for instance, that you are playing dice in a casino that offers single odds and that you wish to put $10 in action every time you bet. Instead of wagering the full $10 on the don't pass line, make a bet of just $5. Then after a point has been established, lay the amount of odds that will enable you to win $5 on your odds wager every time the shooter sevens out.

As an example, if the shooter establishes a point of 8, you would lay the odds for an additional $6. Although you now will have a total of $11 in action instead of the desired $10, you needn't be concerned, as you can expect the shooter to seven-out six times for every five times that he repeats this point number. The 6-to-5 odds in your favor compensate for the larger bet, and as a result, your overall risk is reduced by the desired amount.

Don't Come Bets

A don't come bet is identical to a don't pass line bet, with one exception: A don't come bet may be made on every throw of the dice once the shooter has established a point. To make a don't come bet, you merely place the amount of chips you wish to wager in the designated section of the craps layout.

After you have placed a don't come bet, the very next throw of the dice becomes the come-out roll for that wager. Thus if the shooter rolls a craps number of 2 or 3, you will win while don't pass line bettors will not be affected. If a 7 is rolled, you will lose and wagers on the don't pass line will win. You also will lose if an 11 is thrown, although this number will not have a bearing on don't pass wagers. A roll of 12 is a stand-off; that is, it will have no effect on either your don't come wager or bets on the don't pass line.

Should the shooter throw one of the box numbers on the first roll of the dice after you've made a wager on the don't come, this number becomes an established come point. To win your don't come bet, a 7 must be rolled before the come point is repeated. As an example, if the shooter throws a 10 on the initial roll, he must roll a 7 before repeating the 10 for you to win this wager. Any other numbers rolled in the interim will not affect your don't come bet.

Once a come point has been established, the dealer will move the chips you have wagered on the don't come to a designated spot behind the corresponding numbered box to await a decision on your bet. When you win a don't come bet, the dealer will pay you off by placing your original wager, along with your winnings, in the don't come section of the craps layout. If you do not immediately retrieve your chips, they will be in action on the next roll of the dice as a new don't come bet.

The house advantage on don't come bets is identical to that for don't pass line bets. However, you are allowed to lay the same amount of odds on don't come bets as you are on don't pass wagers, which will have the same effect of reducing the overall house edge on your total wager. To make an odds bet on the don't come, just hand the dealer the appropriate amount of chips and tell him that you wish to lay the odds.

Incidentally, you are permitted to retrieve not only your odds wager, but also your original don't come bet at any time. However, this is not recommended, as once a come point has been established, you have an advantage over the house.

If you make a lot of don't come bets, there will be times when you have most of the numbers on the table covered. This can make the game of craps very exciting — especially when a succession of shooters roll several different box numbers and fail to repeat them before throwing a 7.

However, such fast action can be confusing to a novice player. So if you are new to craps and wish to be a "wrong bettor," we advise that you start out by making a don't pass line bet with odds and one don't come bet with odds. As you gain experience and become more familiar with the game, you can comfortably increase the number of wagers you make on the don't come.

Place Bets on 6 and 8

We've already covered the four best bets that you can make in the game of craps. There are, however, two other reasonably good wagers in terms of the house advantage. These wagers are the place bets on 6 and 8.

A place bet can be made on any of the point numbers (4, 5, 6, 8, 9, or 10) at any time during a hand and is simply a wager that one of these numbers will be rolled before the shooter throws a 7. You cannot take the odds on place bets.

To make a place bet on the 6 or 8, hand your chips to the dealer and ask him to "place the six" or "place the eight." The dealer will then put your wager on the appropriate box number.

Place bets on the 6 and 8 are paid off at 7-to-6 on correct odds of 6-to-5, which gives the casino an advantage of 1.51 percent on these wagers. To ensure that you receive the full 7-to-6 payoff on the 6 and 8, you must make your bet in multiples of six, such as $6, $12, $18, and so forth. For example, if you place the 6 for $18 and win, your $18 original bet will be returned to you, along with an additional $21 in winnings.

As a reminder, any bet where the casino has an advantage is a bet that theoretically will cost you money. Even so, if you make only those wagers that carry a small house edge, your chances of leaving the craps table a winner after a short playing session are reasonably good. We recommend that you make only the following bets, which are the six best wagers in the game of craps:

- Pass line bets with full odds

- Come bets with full odds

- Don't pass bets with full odds

28 Fundamentals of Craps

- Don't come bets with full odds

- Place bet on 6

- Place bet on 8

Other Multiple-Roll Bets

Introduction

Besides the six bets already discussed, there are numerous other wagers available in the game of craps. However, the multiple-roll bets that we deal with in this section, as well as the single-roll bets covered in the section that follows, are not recommended, as we believe the house percentages are too high for these wagers to be a reasonable gamble.

Of course, if you play a lot of craps and always make some of these bets, you can expect to occasionally get lucky and do well. More often, however, you will rapidly deplete your gambling bankroll. Consequently, we have included a discussion of these bets in the *Fundamentals of Craps* for completeness only, not for your consideration, and we again advise you to never make them.

The Remaining Place Bets

In addition to placing bets on the 6 and 8, you also can make place bets on the 4, 5, 9, and 10. A place bet, as noted in the last section, is a wager that a specific point number will be rolled before a 7 is thrown. Place bets on the 5 and 9 have a house advantage of 4.0 percent, as the casino pays 7-to-5 on correct odds of 3-to-2. Place bets on the 4 and 10 are paid off at 9-to-5 on a 2-to-1 shot, which gives the casino an edge of 6.6 percent on these wagers.

To ensure that you receive the full 7-to-5 payoff on the 5 and 9 or the full payoff of 9-to-5 on the 4 and 10, you must make your place bet in multiples of five, such as $5, $10, $25, and so forth. For example, if you place the 9 for $10 and win, your $10 original bet will be returned to you, along with an additional $14 in winnings.

Buy Bets

Another way to cover the numbers — that is, to wager that a particular point (or points) will be rolled before a 7 — is to make buy bets, which are paid off at the correct odds (6-to-5 on the 6 and 8, 3-to-2 on the 5 and 9, and 2-to-1 on the 4 and 10). However, to make this wager, you must pay the casino an extra 5 percent commission when you purchase the bet. The commission — referred to as "vigorish," or "vig" for short — is retained by the house whether you win or lose.

For example, if you wish to buy the 5 for $20, you must give the dealer $21. If you win this bet, you will receive your original $20 back, plus $30 in winnings (paid at correct odds of 3-to-2), but the house will keep the $1 vig.

Because of the 5 percent commission, it is best to make buy bets in multiples of $20 ($20, $40, $60, and so forth). Otherwise, you're likely to be charged the vig applicable to the next higher multiple of $20 anyway, which in turn would have the effect of increasing the casino's edge. Incidentally, although the commission on a buy bet is 5 percent, the house advantage is only 4.7 percent, as the casino is essentially taking $1 out of every $21 that you wager.

Note that it is cheaper in terms of house advantage to buy the 4 and the 10 than it is to place them. However, on the other point numbers, you are better off making place bets.

Big 6 and Big 8 Bets

At the outer corners of the craps layout are two boxes marked with the large figures 6 and 8. This is the space for placing big 6 and big 8 bets, which are wagers that a 6 or an 8 will be rolled before a 7. These bets pay even money, thus giving the house an edge of 9.1 percent.

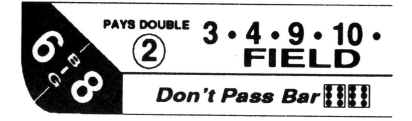

Notice that craps provides three different ways to wager that a 6 or an 8 will come up before a 7 is rolled: place bets with a house edge of 1.5 percent, buy bets with a house edge of 4.7 percent, and wagers on the big 6 and big 8 with a house edge of 9.1 percent. Darwin Ortiz, the author of *On Casino Gambling,* compares this to going to a supermarket that has the same product on sale in three different locations at three different prices. Clearly, if you were going to make this purchase, you would not make it at the highest price. The same principle applies at the dice table.

Lay Bets

A lay bet is the opposite of a buy bet — that is, it is a wager that a 7 will be rolled before a particular point number. However, the 5 percent commission on lay bets is based on the amount of money you have the chance of winning, not on the amount you wager.

For example, suppose you make a lay bet of $40 on the 4. Since lay bets are paid off at the correct odds, which in this case are 1-to-2, you are hoping to win $20 on your wager. Therefore, you must pay the house a commission of $1 at the time you make your bet. The casino retains the 5 percent commission on lay bets, just as it does with buy bets, whether you win or lose.

Because this 5 percent commission is figured on the amount you will win, the house edge varies according to the point number. Thus, lay bets on the 4 and 10 at 1-to-2 odds have a house vig of 2.44 percent; lay bets on the 5 and 9 at 2-to-3 odds have a house edge of 3.22 percent; and lay bets on the 6 and 8 at 5-to-6 odds carry a house advantage of 4 percent.

Hardway Bets

Although hardway bets are actually proposition bets — as opposed to wagers that cover the numbers — we are including them in this section since they usually require more than one roll of the dice before a decision can be determined.

A hardway bet is a wager that a 4, 6, 8, or 10 will be rolled by pairing the dice — that is, by rolling 2-2, 3-3, 4-4, or 5-5 — before either a 7 is thrown or the particular point number comes up the easy way. As an example, suppose you make a hardway bet on the 8. You will win your wager if 4-4 is rolled before 2-6, 6-2, 3-5, 5-3, or any 7; you will lose if one of these number combinations is thrown before 4-4. All other numbers rolled in the interim are disregarded for this wager.

Hardway bets can be made at any time. Just toss your wager to the stickman and tell him that you wish to make this bet. The stickman will then place your wager in the appropriate spot on the center of the craps layout.

HARDWAY BETS

The payoff is 7-to-1 on a hardway bet on the 4 and 10, which produces a house vig of 11.1 percent. Hardway bets on the 6 and 8 are paid at 9-to-1, giving the house an advantage of 9.1 percent. Incidentally, the craps layout shows these payoffs as being 8-for-1 and 10-for-1 respectively, which is just a different way of expressing odds of 7-to-1 and 9-to-1.

One-Roll Bets

Introduction

All of the multiple-roll wagers discussed in the last section — with the exception of hardway bets — have to do with covering the numbers, and the results of these wagers are always contingent on whether a certain number is rolled before a 7, or vice versa. Sometimes these bets are resolved immediately, but at other times, numerous rolls of the dice are required and many irrelevant numbers may appear before the outcome of a wager is determined.

In contrast, when you make a one-roll bet, the outcome of your wager is decided on the very next throw of the dice. These bets offer the fastest action on the craps table, and some players find it very exciting to win or lose on each roll of the dice. However, all of the one-roll bets carry a high house advantage, thus we recommend that you never make them. Even so, we have included a discussion of these wagers in the *Fundamentals of Craps* as they are part of the game.

The Field Bet

On either side of the craps layout is a large rectangle marked with the word "FIELD" and the numbers 2, 3, 4, 9, 10, 11, and 12. This is the space for field bets, which can be made at any time by placing your wager in the rectangle. If a 3, 4, 9, 10, or 11 is thrown on the next roll of the dice, you will be paid off at even money (1-to-1). If either a 2 or a 12 is rolled, the payoff is 2-to-1 — double the amount you wagered. If any other number appears, you will lose your money. This produces an overall house edge of 5.26 percent on field bets.

Many casinos, notably those in downtown Las Vegas and in Northern Nevada, pay triple on a field bet (3-to-1) if a 2 — or in some places, a 12 — is rolled. When this is the case, the house has an overall advantage of 2.56 percent on these wagers. By the way, some casinos have a 5 instead of a 9 on the field space, but this does not change the house edge.

Although the house will pay off on seven of the 11 possible bets that can be rolled, it is actually making payoffs on only 16 of the possible 36 dice combinations. In other words, 20 of the possible combinations will produce a loss for field bets. This is why casinos can offer a 2-to-1 payback on the 2 and 12 — and sometimes a triple payback on one of these numbers — and still show a profit.

Number Bets

The number bets, craps-eleven bet, hop bets, and horn bet, as well as the hardway bets covered in the previous section, are referred to collectively as "proposition bets." These wagers can be made at any time during a craps game.

A number bet is a wager that a 2, 3, 7, 11, or 12 will be thrown on the next roll of the dice. A wager on either 2 or 12 pays 29-to-1 (30-for-1), a wager on either 3 or 11 pays 14-to-1 (15-for-1), and a wager on 7 pays 4-to-1 (5-for-1), giving the house an edge of 16.6 percent on these bets.

You also can bet that any one of the three craps numbers will be rolled. A wager on any craps is paid at 7-to-1 (8-for-1), which produces a house advantage of 11.1 percent.

To make one of these wagers, toss the appropriate amount of chips to the stickman and tell him which bet you wish to make. The stickman will then place your wager in the space provided on the center portion of the craps layout.

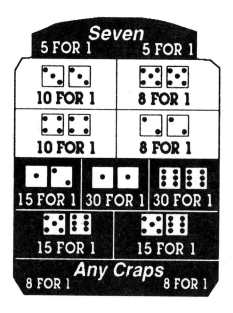

OTHER ONE-ROLL BETS

The C-E Bet

The craps-eleven bet, also known as the C-E bet, is a wager that a 2, 3, 11, or 12 will appear on the next roll of the dice. If a 2, 3, or 12 is thrown, which is craps, the bet is paid off at 3-to-1; if an 11 is rolled, the bet is paid off at 7-to-1. Notice that making the C-E bet is exactly the same as making individual wagers, each for half the amount, on the 11 and on any craps. C-E bets are placed by the stickman in the small designated circles located on either side of the center proposition box.

Hop Bets

A hop bet is a wager that a specific number combination will come up on the next roll of the dice. As an example, if you give the stickman your wager and tell him, "Five-three on the hop" or "Hop five-three," you are betting that the next roll will show 5-3 or 3-5. If any other number combination is thrown, you will lose money.

A hop bet on a pair, which is a wager that an even number will be rolled the hardway (2-2, 3-3, 4-4, and so forth), is paid off at 29-to-1 (30-for-1), giving the house an edge of 16.6 percent. The payoff for hop bets on other number combinations is 14-to-1 (15-for-1), which also provides a house vig of 16.6 percent. Hop bets do not have a designated space on the craps layout.

The Horn Bet

Another bet that does not have a specific space on most craps layouts is the horn bet, which is a wager that a 2, 3, 11, or 12 will appear on the next roll of the dice. The horn bet is actually four different bets, in that you are placing one wager on each of the four numbers. This means that the minimum horn bet is four times the table minimum.

If one of the four numbers comes up on the next roll, you will be paid off at the appropriate odds on one-fourth of your bet and will lose the remaining three-fourths. For instance, suppose you wager $4 on the horn and the shooter rolls a 2. You will lose $3, which accounts for your bets on the 3, 11, and 12. However, your $1 wager on the 2 will be returned to you, along with an additional $29, which represents the 29-to-1 (30-for-1) payoff on the 2.

A variation of the horn bet is the horn high bet. This wager is identical to the horn bet, except that one of the four numbers is designated for a double wager. This means that the horn high bet requires five betting units instead of four. As an example, if you tell the stickman that you wish to wager $5 on "horn high three," you are betting $1 each on 2, 11, and 12 and $2 on the 3. Payoffs on horn high bets are made at the applicable odds for the number rolled.

Other Topics

Introduction

What we've covered in this booklet so far is essentially everything you need to know to play the casino game of craps. Nevertheless, a great deal of information appears in the gaming literature about related topics that some so-called authorities would have you believe are the most important part of gambling. Nothing, however, could be further from the truth. Consequently, the information in this section is very important reading — not because of what it will teach you to do, but because of the traps it may help you avoid.

Money Management Fallacies

Money management is a subject that seems to find its way into the majority of books written on gambling, so it might as well be addressed here. Unfortunately, little of what has been written on this topic is accurate. Though many gaming authors claim that the real secret to gambling success is proper management of your bankroll, one overriding fact needs to be pointed out: If you play a negative-expectation game — and play it long enough — you will lose all of your money.

Unless you are playing a casino game that can be beat, such as poker or blackjack, you should be playing for recreational purposes only. This being said, let's examine a few of the fallacies that constantly crop up under the subject of money management.

Fallacy No. 1: A formula exists that tells you when you have won enough money to quit playing. For most gambling games, formulas *do* exist that tell you how much you can expect to win or lose and what kind of fluctuations to anticipate. But no formula exists that tells you when you have won enough money to cash out. Our advice is this: If you are having a good time at the craps table and want to continue playing, then do so. Otherwise, quit.

Fallacy No. 2: A formula exists that tells you when you have lost enough money to quit playing. The idea of a stop-loss does not mathematically exist. Once you have lost some money, there are many reasons to stop playing. As an example, perhaps you've become tired and are no longer enjoying the game. But there is no stop-loss formula that will let you know when it is time to quit playing.

Fallacy No. 3: Never risk your entire bankroll in one session. Suppose you make a $10 bet. Does it matter whether you have $200 or $2,000 on the table? Of course not. On the other hand, splitting your bankroll into several smaller "session" bankrolls is not incorrect. We consider this a personal matter, and you should do what makes you feel the most comfortable.

Fallacy No. 4: You need some minimum amount of money to play craps. Since craps is a negative-expectation game, if you play it long enough, you will lose all your money no matter how large your bankroll may be. But in the short run, you might get lucky and win. In fact, this occurs fairly often because of the large short-term luck factor present in the game.

This being the case, it doesn't really matter how much money you bring to the craps table. However, keep in mind that the larger your basic betting unit is in relation to your total bankroll, the greater your chance of going broke quickly. Our recommendation is to play at a level you are comfortable with, as we believe the amount of risk that you're willing to take is a personal decision.

How Much
Should You Bet

In beatable games such as blackjack and certain forms of video poker, the question of how much you should bet is very important, assuming you have the skill to win. There are two reasons for this. The first is that if you bet too small, you won't win enough in the long run. This should be obvious since each time you make a bet, you theoretically earn a small percentage of your wager that corresponds to your edge over the casino.

The second reason is just the opposite: If your bets are too large, even though you have an edge over the casino, you can put your gambling bankroll in jeopardy and even lose. To understand this, take the extreme example of always betting all your money. Even though you may have the best of it, you don't expect to win every bet, and if all your money is always at risk, you can anticipate going broke when you finally hit that losing bet.

Consequently, serious gamblers who have the skill to beat certain games are very concerned with bet sizing. Furthermore, mathematical formulas are available that can help determine the proper size bet, but these formulas are beyond the scope of this book.

Craps, however, is different because it is *not* a beatable game, and those mathematical bet-sizing formulas apply only to games that can be beat. Simply put, if you play craps long enough, you can expect to lose. Of course, because there is much short-term luck in craps, as there is in many other forms of gambling, you can be ahead after a short session, or even after several short sessions. That's why we have emphasized the good bets that are available on the craps table and taking the odds, and why we state that craps is a good gamble. By sticking to what we recommend, you are more likely to be ahead after a short period of time than if you were to make some of the high house percentage wagers, such as the proposition bets located in the center of the table. But always keep in mind that the more you play, the more likely it is that you will be a loser.

This brings us to our answer to the question of how much you should bet. Craps should be viewed as a form of entertainment. It may be very exciting to play with the action coming at a fast and furious pace, but it is still entertainment. Thus the amount to bet should simply be an amount that you are comfortable with. It might also be an amount that you find somewhat stimulating in the sense that if you do win, you'll be happy about the win.

Finally, we want to address one more misconception that you often hear when at a gambling destination. It is the idea that you should bet more with the casino's money than with your own.

What is meant by this is that if you happen to be ahead, there is no risk on the money that you have won, since it didn't belong to you when you started. That is, if you lose this money back, it would be like you never played in the first place. Therefore, in a sense it is free money and there is no need to hoard it, so you should feel free to bet it at a higher rate.

Of course, casinos love advice like this, since they know that theoretically they earn a small percentage corresponding to the house edge on every wager that is made. Furthermore, the more you bet, the higher their expected earn is. So casinos hope to entice you to bet more, as their long-term profit is enhanced.

The answer here is that "casino money" is really a fictitious idea. Any money that you have won is your money and belongs to no one else, and it especially does not belong to the casino. It's also easy to see this. Just cash in your winnings and spend that extra money on something you want.

Some Thoughts on Systems

In general, most systems we see recommended in the gambling literature are not worth much, as they are related only to how you bet and your previous results. Nothing else is taken into consideration.

In certain gambling games, such as blackjack, some systems do show a long-term profit if used correctly. They do this by identifying when you have the advantage instead of the casino. Unfortunately, no system like this exists for the game of craps.

All craps systems come under the heading of betting systems, which usually recommend that you bet more when losing in an effort to recover your losses. This presents a serious problem. If you have a prolonged losing streak — and the laws of probability state that if you play craps long enough, you eventually will get unlucky and have a prolonged losing streak — you will get wiped out.

Another author on this subject put it this way: "If someone says he has a great system, tell him he can't borrow any money six months from now." We agree completely.

In the past few years, a new type of system has appeared in some of the craps literature. It is based on the idea that tables can run hot and cold in predictable patterns and claims that you can take advantage of this phenomenon. All you have to do is watch to see whether a table is exceptionally hot or cold and then bet in the appropriate manner.

The fact is, there is a tremendous amount of short-term luck in craps. This means that in a large casino containing many craps tables, there is bound to be a table where the shooter, in some recent period of time, has made many more passes than what normally would be expected, or where some of the proposition bettors have hit their numbers much more frequently than the odds dictate they should. However, there is no reason to believe this pseudo trend will continue.

If at some time in the future you are tempted to purchase a craps system — which is usually very expensive — our advice is to save your money. Despite claims to the contrary, these systems won't improve your long-term results.

Also, there is no such thing as a professional craps player. In games like poker and blackjack, which can be beat, there are professional players. But this is not the case in craps. Anyone who states that he is a professional or that he has a method that wins at craps in the long run either is not being truthful or is playing the game in a dishonest fashion.

Oscar's Grind

Although we've emphasized that system play does not improve your results, we will introduce you to one system. Known as Oscar's Grind, this system was first described in 1965 by Allan Wilson in his classic book *The Casino Gambler's Guide*.

"This system," wrote Wilson, "is designed so that in each sequence of plays, the player gains a net profit of one unit and then starts over again." Oscar's Grind works like this. You start out by betting one unit. If you lose a bet, your next bet is the same size as the one just lost. If you win a bet, your next bet is one unit larger, unless you win a bet that will produce a profit greater than one unit for the sequence. In this case, you reduce your bet size to an amount that is just large enough to produce a profit of exactly one unit.

What is unique about this system is that the profit is held down to one unit per each successful sequence. Some professed craps authorities will advise you to let your profits maximize when the table is hot. This system will do almost exactly the opposite.

Following is an example of Oscar's Grind in action:

- You start out by betting one unit and lose. You are now down by one unit.

- You again bet one unit and lose again. You are now down by two units.

- You again bet one unit, which wins. You are now down by one unit.

- Since you won the last bet, you bet two units and lose. You are now down by three units.

- You bet two units again and win. You are now down by one unit.

- You bet two units for a third time and win. Your sequence is now complete, as you have made a profit of *exactly* one unit.

It seems as though you can't lose if you follow Oscar's Grind, and it's true that you can play with a moderate bankroll for very long periods of time before you fail to complete a sequence. But if you use this system long enough, there's no doubt that eventually you will not complete a sequence. You will either run out of money or run up against the house betting limit. When this happens, your results are catastrophic.

Note that the house edge remains the same whether you use this betting system or any other. For example, if you are making pass line bets, the house advantage is 1.41 percent whether you are following Oscar's Grind, adhering to some other betting system, or just wagering haphazardly.

Nevertheless, using Oscar's Grind will enable you to almost always leave the table a winner. In fact, it can be a lot of fun to take a friend to the craps table and assure him that you will walk away a winner, and the vast majority of the time that will be the case. But keep in mind that when you fail to win, which on occasion will happen, your results will be — what was that word? — catastrophic.

Crapless Craps

Wouldn't it be nice if you couldn't crap out on the first roll? That is, if you roll a 2, 3, or 12, it is simply your point and you no longer automatically lose. Well, there is a game like this. It is called "crapless craps," and it is offered by a small number of casinos.

There is one other difference in crapless craps: If you roll an 11, this is also a point rather than an automatic win, while a 7 on the come-out role still wins.

At first it seems that the rules for this game are actually better for the player than the rules of standard craps, since you are helped on three possible rolls and hurt only on one. Unfortunately, this is not the case.

The reason is that you are not helped much when the come out-roll is a 2, 3, or 12. That's because you will only rarely make your point when you roll one of these numbers. For example, if 2 is your point, you are six times more likely to roll a 7 than a 2. Compare this to a point of 8, where the 7 is only a 6-to-5 favorite over the 8.

But you are hurt quite a bit when the come-out roll is an 11, since now you will win only 25 percent of the time as opposed to winning all the time. This makes all the difference in the world and is much more significant than what most people think, especially those who are not familiar with this game.

It turns out that the house edge is a whopping 5.4 percent. This compares to 1.4 percent for the standard craps game. So unlike standard craps, crapless craps by our criteria would not be considered a good bet.

However, those casinos that offer crapless craps usually allow the bettor to make a very large multi-odds bet. When this is the case, the house edge can be brought down to a reasonable percentage. In fact, you will have a few more opportunities to take the odds at crapless craps since there are more points to be made. Thus odds bets can help you even more in this game than in standard craps. This means that crapless craps is not such a bad gamble after all.

Casino Comps

Casinos expect to win, and most of their customers expect the casinos to win. Of course, both parties know that on any given night the outcome can be different, but in general the money goes to the house. If this weren't the case, there wouldn't be so many casinos, and they wouldn't be built as lavishly as most of them are.

To help compensate for their advantage, and to make your gambling experience more enjoyable and thus encourage you to come back for another visit and another turn at the gambling tables, virtually all casinos offer comps to their better customers. These comps can include food — which can range from a small discount at a snack bar to a fabulous gourmet meal in a terrific restaurant — free rooms, free shows with great seats, transportation refunds, special parties for invited guests, and passes to other casino attractions.

Generally, casinos figure that the typical player will lose approximately 1.5 percent to 2 percent of his total betting action, and they are willing to return a portion of this to ensure that their customers' gambling experience is as enjoyable as possible. Sometimes as much as 30 percent to 40 percent of your expected loss can be redeemed in this way.

Now, that 1.5 percent to 2 percent may not seem like much, but in time it can add up, especially in a fast-paced game like craps. So the casino can afford to treat you well.

But notice that when playing craps, if you master the techniques described in this book, you should be playing with a much smaller house edge than 1.5 percent to 2 percent. Now add in a few comps, and your true mathematical expectaion may be to lose very little.

Usually, what will happen when you begin a craps session, unless you are playing for very small stakes, is that the supervisor at the table will ask if you would like to be rated. If you answer in the affirmative the supervisor will watch and track your play and estimate your average bet size. That, plus the length of time that you play, will determine what comps you may be eligible for.

If you bet small and take large odds bets, the pit boss should recognize that you are not really giving that much action, since the house has no edge on the odds. However, if you mix up your bets a little and the table is busy, you may get rated for betting more on average than you really do. So the comps may still be available to you.

Some casinos may want to issue you a "playing card" that identifies you with a tracking number. If you are interested in receiving any comps, accept this card and present it every time you play in this particular casino. The casino will now have a record of your total action and can fully reward you for your play.

In addition, a host may introduce himself to you and present you with his personal business card. This will enable you to call him any time, and he can issue you a comp even when you are not in the casino. It will be there waiting for you to arrive.

Finally, we advise you not to be shy. When you are playing or just after you've concluded a session, the best way to receive a comp is to ask for one. It's true that on occasion a casino host might introduce himself and invite you to "dinner on the house," but usually you need to initiate the action.

By the way, we want to add a special caution concerning comps and craps. Skillful players in some games, such as blackjack, can reduce the house edge to almost nothing and even occasionally have a positive expectation. But this will hardly ever be the case in craps no matter how skillful you play. The game is not beatable, and if casino personnel are doing their jobs well, you will be required to truly earn your comps.

Of course, this doesn't mean that you shouldn't ask for comps or should not play craps. But it does mean that if you are going to a casino and playing solely for the purpose of earning comps, there are better games to choose. It also means that if you like to make some of those proposition bets, the comps that you receive can be very expensive.

A Craps Quiz

We have covered a great deal of material in the *Fundamentals of Craps*. To see whether you have absorbed it all and will know what to do at the dice table, we have prepared a short quiz for you. Good luck.

1. What is the house advantage on an odds bet?

    There is no house advantage on an odds bet. This is true whether you are taking or laying the odds.

2. What is a wrong bet?

    It is a wager that the shooter will lose.

3. What is a place bet?

    A place bet is a wager that one of the totals represented by a point box will be rolled before a 7 is thrown.

4. What effect do betting systems have on the house advantage?

    They have absolutely no effect on the house advantage. Despite what you may hear, your long-term results are unaffected by any betting system.

5. What is the reverse of a buy bet?

    A lay bet is the reverse of a buy bet; that is, you are wagering that a 7 will be rolled before a particular point number.

6. What is a hop bet?

    A hop bet is a wager that each die will show a specific number on the next roll.

7. How should you bet when playing the pass line?

First, you should determine how much money you want to put in action on each bet. Then bet enough on the pass line so that this wager, plus the maximum allowed odds bet, will equal the total amount you want to put in action. Then, when a point is established, go ahead and make the maximum odds bet.

8. What is the advantage of betting this way?

You get the desired amount of money in action at the lowest possible house advantage.

9. What is the pass line bet?

The pass line bet is an even money wager that wins for you when the shooter rolls a total of 7 or 11 on the come-out roll, or when he rolls a 4, 5, 6, 8, 9, or 10 on the come-out roll and repeats this number before he throws a 7. The bet loses for you if the come-out roll is a 2, 3, or 12, or when a 7 is rolled before the established point number is repeated.

10. Why was the bar-12 rule established for a don't pass line bet?

It was established to ensure that the house has an advantage. If this rule did not exist, the player would be getting the best of it.

11. If you want to cover the number 6, what is the worst way to do it?

By making the big 6 bet. The house advantage on this wager is 9.1 percent.

12. After you establish a point, what happens when you roll a number that is not your point number or a 7?

Nothing happens if you have a wager on the pass line. However, this number may affect other bets on the craps layout.

13. What are the six best bets in craps?

They are (1) pass line bets with full odds, (2) come bets with full odds, (3) don't pass bets with full odds, (4) don't come bets with full odds, (5) the place bet on 6, and (6) the place bet on 8.

14. Does a formula exist that tells you when you have won enough money to quit playing?

No, despite what you may read or hear to the contrary.

15. To bet the pass line, do you have to be the shooter?

No. Anyone can bet the pass line. But if you are the shooter, you must bet either the pass line or the don't pass line.

16. How does a come bet differ from a pass line bet?

A come bet can be made only after the shooter has established a point.

17. Which place bets are considered low house percentage bets?

Place bets on the 6 and 8. The house edge on these wagers is only 1.51 percent.

18. How often will a 7 be rolled?

There are 36 possible number combinations that can be rolled, and six of these combinations will produce a total of 7. Thus a 7 will be rolled one-sixth of the time.

19. How does the house advantage differ between pass and don't pass bets?

For practical purposes, there is no difference. The house advantage on the pass line is 1.41 percent, and the house advantage on the don't pass line is 1.40 percent.

20. Is it possible to win at craps in the long run?

    No, as you cannot consistently beat a purely mechanical game that has a built-in house advantage.

Conclusion

In the *Fundamentals of Craps*, we have attempted to provide you with a sound strategy for playing the popular casino game of craps. However, you must keep in mind that craps is a negative-expectation game. In other words, if you play dice long enough, you will lose. On the other hand, there is a lot of short-term luck in craps, which means that by gambling intelligently, you will have a reasonable chance of leaving the table after a short playing session with more chips than you started with.

We strongly suggest that you stick with the bets we have recommended. By making only those wagers that have a low house percentage, you should be able to play longer with any given amount of money, and you will have a greater opportunity of leaving the table a winner after a short session.

Finally, have fun playing craps. Although it is impossible to consistently beat the game in the long run, casino craps is fast and exciting and offers a pleasurable gaming experience.

Glossary

Action: The total amount of money that is bet over a period of time.

Bar: To disallow a specific number. Usually the number 12, but sometimes the number 2, is declared a stand-off on don't bets. If this were not done, players would have an advantage over the house on these wagers.

Bet: A wager made by a player.

Bet with the dice: A bet that the shooter will win.

Big 6 or big 8: A bet made on either a 6 or an 8 that this number will be rolled before a 7. Big 6 and big 8 wagers pay even money.

Boxcars: A total of 12 (6-6).

Boxman: The casino employee who supervises the craps game and handles all monetary transactions.

Box numbers: The six point numbers (4, 5, 6, 8, 9, and 10).

Buck: A round marker used to indicate the point number and to show that the odds are off on the come-out roll; also called a "puck."

Buy bet: A wager that a particular box number will be rolled before a 7 is thrown. The house charges a commission of 5 percent on these bets.

Chip: A token used in place of currency in a casino. Chips also are referred to as "checks."

Come bet: The same as a pass line bet, except that a come bet can be made only after the shooter has established a point.

Come-out roll: The first roll after a line decision.

Come-point: The number (4, 5, 6, 8, 9, or 10) that a shooter must roll before rolling a seven in order to win his bet.

Comp: A complimentary service, such as a free meal or show, given to a preferred customer.

Crapless craps: A version of craps in which 2, 3, 11, and 12 count as point numbers.

Dice: Plural of die.

Die: A small, six-sided cube marked with spots that represent the numbers one through six.

Don't come bet: The same as a don't pass bet, except that a don't come bet can be made only after the shooter has established a point.

Don't pass bet: A wager that the shooter will lose.

Double odds: An odds bet made at twice the amount of the original pass line wager.

Easy way: Rolling a 4, 6, 8, or 10 without pairing the dice; for example, rolling a 3 and a 5 for a total of 8.

Even money: Odds of 1-to-1.

Field bet: A wager that the next roll of the dice will total 2, 3, 4, 9, 10, 11, or 12.

Full odds: The maximum amount that can be bet on the odds relative to the original bet.

Hardway: Pairing the dice on a roll to make a 4, 6, 8, or 10; for example, rolling a pair of 5s for a total of 10.

Hop bet: A wager that a particular number combination will appear on the next roll of the dice.

Horn bet: A proposition bet that the next roll of the dice will total 2, 3, 11, or 12. These wagers must be in multiples of four times the minimum bet.

Horn high bet: A bet similar to the horn bet, except that wagers must be in multiples of five units, with two betting units designated on one of the numbers (2, 3, 11, or 12).

Hot hand: A succession of passes.

House edge: The mathematical advantage the casino has on a bet.

Inside numbers: The 5, 6, 8, and 9.

Lay bet: A wager that a 7 will be thrown before a particular point number is rolled. The house charges a 5 percent commission on these bets.

Layout: The playing surface of a craps table that illustrates the various betting options available.

Long hand: Describes the situation where a shooter rolls many numbers before he either makes his point or sevens-out.

Monster hand: An exceptionally long "hot hand."

Natural: A 7 or an 11 on the come-out roll.

Odds bet: An additional wager either that the point number will be rolled before a 7 — known as taking the odds — or that a 7 will be made before the point number, which is referred to as laying the odds. This is the only bet at the craps table that is paid off at the correct odds.

Off: To remove a bet for one or more rolls.

One-roll bet: Any wager that is settled on the next roll of the dice.

Outside numbers: The 4, 5, 9, and 10.

Pass: A winning decision for pass line bettors.

Pass line: The space on a craps layout where bets are placed wagering that the shooter will win.

Place bet: A wager that a specific box number will be rolled before a 7.

Point: Any of the numbers 4, 5, 6, 8, 9, or 10 when thrown on the come-out roll.

Point numbers: The numbers 4, 5, 6, 8, 9, and 10; also referred to as "box numbers."

Proposition bet: A high house percentage bet that is usually resolved in one roll of the dice.

Right bettor: A player who wagers that the shooter will win; a pass line bettor.

Seven-out: Throwing a 7 before rolling the point number that has been established.

Shoot: To roll the dice. Also, the shooter's total series of rolls.

Shooter: The player who is rolling the dice.

Single odds: The standard odds bet.

Snake eyes: A total of 2 (1-1).

Stick: The wooden stick used by the stickman to move the dice.

Stickman: The casino employee who directs the craps game and sets its pace.

System: A method of betting.

Toke: A tip.

Vigorish: The house percentage or commission; also called "vig."

Wrong bettor: A player who wagers that the shooter will lose; a don't pass line bettor.

Recommended Reading

The purpose of this booklet is to provide you with basic information for playing the casino game of craps. It is not designed to make you an expert player. As emphasized earlier, it is impossible to become an expert at craps, as you cannot consistently beat a purely mechanical game that has a built-in house advantage. Nevertheless, if you are interested in learning more about casino craps, following is a list of some excellent gambling books that discuss this popular game in greater detail.

- *Getting the Best of It* by David Sklansky

- *Gambling for a Living* by David Sklansky and Mason Malmuth

- *The Casino Gambler's Guide* by Allan N. Wilson

- *On Casino Gambling* by Darwin Ortiz

- *The Mathematics of Games and Gambling* by Edward Packel

Index